Surviving War in No-Man's Land

By

Henry Kuznik

This is a work of non-fiction. Names, characters, places, and incidents are neither the product of the author's imagination nor are they used fictitiously unless otherwise noted.

Surviving War in No-Man's Land

Printing history: 1st edition, 2nd printing/ May 2016 All rights reserved.
Copyright © March 2016

ISBN-13: 978-0692678176 (Kuznik Publishing)
ISBN-10: 0692678174

7290 Investment Drive,
Suite B
North Charleston, SC 29418

PRINTED IN THE UNITED STATES OF AMERICA

Edited by Debbie G. Brownfield

Dedication

This book is dedicated to those noble people on all sides who gave their lives both fighting in and living through World War II.

iv

Contents

Chapter One
Froghoppers!

Trouble should have been my middle name. On New Year's Eve each year, we had many small firecrackers in Germany.

One such firecracker was called a "froghopper." We would light one end of it, and it would hop every couple of seconds about two feet into the air, eight or ten times.

The older boys would drop one of the froghoppers on a girl's shoe, and it would hop up under her dress. We would laugh so hard when the girls jumped and screamed.

One year a few days after New Year's Day, I found a froghopper in the grass on the way to school. It had been lit but had not hopped, and it was still in one piece. I picked it up and put it into my pants' pocket.

After school while at Grandma's house, I took it out of my pocket and went to the back of the house where no one could see me. The froghopper had a string attached, and each time it hopped, some of the string broke off. I lit it and threw it onto the ground.

When it did not hop, I picked it up and straightened it. Nothing happened. So I picked it up—it was in the shape of a tube—and looking into the burned end, saw that it was still smoldering. I blew into it, and it exploded in my face!

I started screaming and running toward the house to find my grandmother. I fell twice, once over a stone and then over a hand wagon.

By the time I had hit the ground, my grandmother was beside me. My mother, who was working at the factory, heard me screaming, and everyone came to see what had happened.

My face was black from the powder, and I could not see. My mother and grandmother got me by the arms and led me inside the house. They asked me what had happened, but all I could do was cry and say my eyes hurt and I could not see.

They saw that both of my eyes were full of powder. They washed my face and tried to clean my eyes. They could not get the powder out, and the more I blinked the more my eyes hurt.

So they wrapped a thin dish towel around my eyes and took me to a regular doctor. After examining my eyes with a magnifying glass, he said that he could not help. They would have to take me to a specialist. He put some ointment in my eyes and patches over both.

That same day they took me to the specialist. We had to take the train to Katowice which was approximately sixty miles away. At that time, very few eye specialists existed.

After the specialist examined me, he told my mother that I might be blind in both eyes and that one eye was worse than the other. He cleaned the powder out of my eyes, put some ointment in them, and put the patches back in place.

Although he had removed all of the powder, my eyes would need time to heal. He wanted to see me twice a week.

The trip took an hour and a half one way because the train had to make so many stops. It was a steam locomotive fired by wood and coal and could not go very fast. I had to be led everywhere, a dreary prospect for a small boy.

After a month, I only needed a patch on one eye. I could see out of the other although it was very blurry. My visits to the doctor decreased to once a week, and after six months, my eyes were much better, and I did not have to go back to him anymore. However, I still have to put drops in both eyes, and I want nothing to do with fireworks to this day!

Chapter Two
My Parents before the War

The Soppa sisters, Terese, Lucy and Heidl, were smelly. That was a fact. The family owned a fish and cheese distributorship, and the job of the sisters was to smoke the dried fish. The brothers, Karl and Thomas, had other responsibilities.

Thomas was in school and spoke four different languages—Russian, French, German, and Polish. When the war came, he was used as an interpreter on the Russian front. He was wounded in the war and had shrapnel in his head and, at times, severe memory loss.

Karl helped in the business and sometimes drove one of the delivery trucks, taking merchandise from the factory to the grocery stores. One time, he fell asleep at the wheel and hit a tree. He cried and contacted his mother telling her about the accident and that the truck could not be driven.

The girls were responsible for making sure that the sawdust in the bottom of the smoker did not catch fire. The smoker was a pit, about four feet by three feet, ten feet tall with divided steel doors on the top and the bottom.

The bottom doors could be opened to check the sawdust smoke, and the top doors opened to the place where the fish, skewered through the eyes, were hung to be smoked. A wire mesh between each layer of fish kept them from falling into the sawdust and catching fire.

Yes, the three Soppa sisters were smelly. If one or all of them went to the movies or a dance, the surrounding people knew that at least one of them was not far away. They could smell them before they could see them. Not even a long bath could remove the smell!

They all went to dances frequently because their father, Grossvater Soppa, loved to dance, but many of the men would not ask the sisters to dance because of the smoky smell.

Yes, the Soppa sisters were smelly, but they were also pretty.

One night, my father, Bruno, told his friends that he was going to get one of the smelly girls to dance with him. He asked my mother to dance with him, and, after a few dances, they had fallen in love!

Six months later, Bruno asked Terese to marry him. She said "Yes!" She was only sixteen years old!

Because Lucy was getting married, too, they decided to have a double wedding. Grossvater Soppa was so proud! He was a well-known and well-liked businessman, and everyone wanted to attend and offer their good wishes to both couples.

So Grossvater prepared for a large wedding and a sit-down banquet to follow. Between one hundred and fifty to two hundred guests sat down at the feast.

Following tradition, one of the bride's shoes was auctioned to the highest bidder, and the groom had to buy it back. Then he had to drink wine out of the shoe.

Another tradition was that a gentleman guest would steal the bride when the groom was not looking. He would take the bride from one pub to another, running up tabs that the groom had to pay to redeem his bride.

With two brides to kidnap, the wedding celebration lasted two to three days with dancing and music the whole time. It was a festive, happy affair.

*****

My dad bought a small house on the outskirts of town with the help of his parents. The house had a living room, kitchen, bathroom, and two bedrooms. Surrounded by farmland and pastureland, it was an idyllic setting.

Two large willow trees on the bank of a pond in front of the house hung their leaves gracefully in the water, and on one side a shallow brook with clean, fresh water meandered slowly past.

A farmer owned the adjoining farm in back of the house, and in the distance was his herd of cows and a flock of domestic geese. Wildflowers growing in the fields completed the serene setting.

On July 24, 1933, I was born in this serene, peaceful atmosphere, the first child of some very excited parents and the first grandchild of some very proud grandparents, especially Grossvater! I was a BOY!

One morning before I was a year old, my mother gave me a warm bath. After my bath, she dried me and put me on a table between two pillows so I would not roll off. It was a fine summer day, so she left me uncovered on the table while she opened the windows for cross ventilation.

Later, however, I developed a high fever, so she took me to the doctor. He determined I had developed pneumonia in both lungs. Because no fever-reducing medication had been developed for children at that time, he could do nothing to help.

In frantic tears, my mother ran with me to my grandmother Soppa who racked her brains to think of someone who might know of some solution. She remembered an old woman, about seventy or eighty years of age, who had some knowledge of home remedies.

The old woman told my grandma to get some rhubarb leaves and crush the large veins. Soak the leaves in cold buttermilk and wrap me completely, including my feet, in the leaves. Then she should wrap me completely and tightly, first in a blanket and then in a down-feather comforter so that I would perspire.

My mother followed her instructions carefully, and approximately twenty-four hours later, my fever had broken, I had stopped crying, and I had fallen into a deep sleep.

A few days later, mother took me back to the doctor. He could not believe my improved condition as he had given up on me. My mother proceeded to explain what she had done, and he was amazed at the results.

Chapter Three
A Fascination with Trains

When I was approximately four years old, my mother and grandmother took me to the train station. My grandma had to leave on a business trip.

The half mile trip took us down a gravel road, through a flower park, and past the bus station to get to the train station. The flower park had wooden benches with trash cans near each one, a good-sized lake with willow and birch trees around it, and many flowers. It was truly a beautiful park.

When we finally reached the train station, my grandma bought her ticket and boarded the train. She waved goodbye as the train left the station.

I was standing at the fence, totally fascinated by the locomotive, the steam it produced, and its whistle. When my mother tried to pry me away to go home, I howled and screamed. I wanted to stay and watch the trains come and go. To calm me, my mother promised she would bring me to the train station when Grandma returned from her trip.

A short time later while playing outside, I decided to go to the train station by myself. So I walked down the long, gravel road past two houses and a farm.

I started through the park, and midway an older lady was sitting on one of the benches by the lake, feeding the ducks. She noticed I was walking alone, so she asked me if I was lost.

I confidently told her no, that I was going to the train station to get my grandma.

She asked me if I knew the way.

"Oh, yes," I said. "I know the way." I had to go the rest of the way through the park, past the bus station, and then I would come to the train station.

My story sounded plausible to her, and she let me continue on my journey.

Once at the station, I found the exact place I had stood by the fence when my grandmother had left on her trip. Close by was a road that the train tracks crossed.

As the trains, loaded with coal, approached the crossing, they had to blow their whistles several times to warn the people because, at that time, no warning lights had been installed. I was mesmerized by the sound of the whistles!

After about an hour, my mother missed me and was terrified. She contacted my dad in town and told him that I was missing. He came home immediately, and they both began searching around the lake in front of the house.

Dad probed the lake with a pole, searching for my body, but found nothing. Next, my parents searched opposite sides of the brook. After checking all around and not finding me, they decided I had wandered toward town.

They contacted the neighbors, and everyone began looking for me! They soon reached the park, and one of the neighbors asked the old lady if she had seen a little boy walking through the park by himself.

She said that yes, she had asked me if I was lost, but I had confidently told her I was going to the train station to meet my grandma and that I knew the way.

My parents raced to the station, and there I was, standing by the fence where I had been the last time. They both hugged and kissed me, and then I got my bottom spanked!

They told me I had better never do that again and that grandma had already returned. My mother kept a closer eye on me, but, as usual, I found more mischief to do!

Chapter Four
Nails!

One day when I was about five years old, my sister and I were left home alone, and I was supposed to be taking care of her.

Most of the time, we would play cards together. Several days earlier, however, my dad had bought a large box of eight-penny nails for a fence he was planning to build.

I was tired of playing cards all the time, so I decided to do something different. I saw the box of nails in a corner of the kitchen, sitting on the floor.

I found a hammer and decided to drive the nails into the cracks between the tongue-and-groove floor planks. During the winter, the wooden floor would dry, and the planks would separate, leaving a small crack.

With my sister handing me the nails, I began at the front door, and I started nailing! I pounded them into the flooring about three to four inches apart the entire length of each plank. I nailed until I had finished the entire entry and living room floors!

Several hours later, my parents returned, but they were unable to even open the door! Finally, my dad forced the door, bending some of the nails.

My parents stared in disbelief, nearly having a heart attack when they saw all I had done in such a short amount of time. No one could walk anywhere because I had nailed my sister and me into another room.

They finally arrived in the room, but they had to step on top of the nails, bending them with each step. It took my dad a long time to pull each nail from the planks, and each nail left a permanent mark in the flooring, a reminder of my misdemeanor.

Here came my dad with the belt, and I had to do extra chores as punishment for that one!

*****

So I grew up mainly around adults because we lived on the outskirts of town, and we did not have many children with whom to play.

In the fall when the potatoes were harvested, everyone had to help, including my grandma's employees because Grandma always fed them lunch. The potatoes were always dug up on the weekends when Grandma's drivers were off work, and the children were out of school.

Seven or eight children from the neighborhood came, and we, as children, had the most fun!

After the larger potatoes were gathered, we children would collect the smaller ones that were left by raking them together. We would also gather the potato stalks.

Then we would dig a pit and put the stalks in it, and Grandma would start a fire for us. We put in the potatoes to roast, and when they were done, we would eat them.

They were so good! Our faces, lips, and clothing became black from the burned potato crusts. Sometimes the crusts were as much as an eighth of an inch thick.

The potatoes that were too burned to eat could then be used like charcoal with which we could write on wood or stone and also paint our arms, legs, and faces.

Next to the potato field was a large grassy field, and Grandma had nearly thirty geese. My job was to let them out each morning to graze and then put them up in the evening. The only way that I could get them back into the coop was to take some feed, and they would come in to eat.

Around this same time, we moved about a quarter of a mile from our old house into town. Our apartment was on the second story of a four-story building across the street from Grandma's factory.

One winter, with about two feet or more of fresh-fallen snow, my sister and I decided to run barefooted to Grandma's house across the street and next to the factory. When we arrived, our feet were red and tingling. She was upset with us and scolded us because she feared we would surely catch a cold.

We had to immediately put on a pair of Grandma's slippers. Then Mother had to go to our apartment and bring us some socks and shoes.

Sometimes, we ate lunch at Grandma's before her employees came for lunch. She had a large wooden table with two benches that sat six people each.

A lot of times we had soup with tough, bite-sized pieces of meat. My sister and I did not care for the meat, so we would suck out the juice. Then, unseen by anyone, we would spit the meat into our hands and throw it between the wall and the bench. We did finally get caught after the meat started rotting and smelling!

We always had to clean our plates, and then we would get a treat. Our treat was sugar that was melted in a pan and made into candy. It was so good!

20

Chapter Five
Grandmother Kuznik and School Days

A few times a month, my mother would take us to visit my father's mother, Grandmother Kuznik. She lived in a two-story house several miles from us. Her house was close to some woods and a big lake. In the summer, I liked to play outside around the lake. In the winter, the lake froze over, and we would ice skate on it.

Grossvater Kuznik was a coal miner all of his life. He was involved in an explosion and was buried under the coal. Some other men were killed, but he made it.

His head had been crushed, and the doctors had to put a steel plate in his head. He also had permanent black spots on his skin. He lost his nose and only had a hole on top so that he could breath.

Grandmother Kuznik cared for him until he passed away in his eighties. I enjoyed visiting them, but, again, was followed by mischief wherever I went.

One afternoon in early spring, the ice on the lake had started to melt, and a three-inch layer of water was on top of the ice. A few kids came to the lake with their sleds. They got on their sleds, and with some ski sticks, pushed themselves around the lake.

I was on the shore watching them enviously. They asked me if I would like to take a ride. Of course I said, "Yes!"

Altogether, were three different sleds. Unbeknownst to us, someone had cut large blocks of ice out of the lake before it had started melting. These blocks were put in sawdust, chilling it, to help keep food from spoiling in the summertime.

Because the water was on top of the ice, we did not notice the large area where the ice had been cut out. The sled on which I was sitting went into the hole, and both of us on the sled landed in the water.

Fortunately, the water was not more than three feet deep. However, I was sitting at the front of the sled, so I went up under the ice. The other boy, who could stand up with his head above the water saw me, hauled me out, and lifted me on top of the ice.

Soaking wet and freezing, we ran to Grandmother Kuznik's house. When Grandma Kuznik opened the door and saw us looking like two drowned, freezing rats, she made us take off our clothes and shoes outside and asked what had happened. She gave us some towels with which to dry ourselves before we could come in the house. Then she shooed us inside and had us get under the feather comforters on her big bed to get warm.

I guess we made a lot of work for her that day because she had to put our shoes next to the fireplace to dry, rinse our clothes, wring them as best she could, and iron them dry. She wanted to make sure that when my mother came to get me that my clothes were good and dry. She also had to notify the other boy's mother.

*****

On the first day of school of a child's first year, each parent sent their child to school with a large, cone-shaped bag filled with cookies and candy.

This was a tradition, and each child was proud to show off his or her bag which

24

was usually twenty to thirty inches long. The children shared their goodies with each other.

Parents, usually the mother, walked their children to and from school each day. My mother walked with me, too, and I remember some children crying when they were left.

After the first year, we walked to school by ourselves which was only about a half a mile down the road. Between forty-five and fifty children were in each class, boys and girls together.

Two grades were in one classroom; girls were seated on one side of the room and boys on the other. The school yard was also divided by a known line that all of us kids knew. The teachers walked back and forth and observed the children.

When recess was over, and the children were back in class, the teachers would call out offending children and bring them in front of the class. Depending on the severity of the offense, the boys would get three or four spanks on their butts, and the girls would get three or four slaps on the palms of their hands with a half inch wide and two foot long switch.

The biggest and tallest boy, known as the bully, would pick on the smallest boy, always. The gates to the school were steel, and one day the bully was challenged to stick his tongue on the gate and take off.

Poor boy, innocent as he was, did not realize that, since it was winter and very cold, his tongue would get stuck. The children laughed, knowing what would happen. The teacher had to go outside and pour hot water on the gate where he was stuck to get his tongue loose.

26

Chapter Six
Grandma Soppa and Her Factory

Grossvater Soppa passed away at the age of thirty-six, and my grandmother was left to run the fish and cheese business by herself. She had several trucks that daily delivered the cheese and fish to various stores within a twenty-mile radius.

At that time, Swiss cheese came in circular loaves that weighed two hundred pounds each. They were rolled into the factory and cut into ten-pound loaves and sold to the stores.

The waxy coating on the twelve to fifteen different types of cheese loaves created a rainbow display of colors, and the various colored waxes kept the cheese loaves fresh.

The hand cheese came in small, wooden boxes so that the cheese could "breathe." Made from overly matured cottage cheese, this hand cheese had a very pungent odor, but it tasted very good once it got past the nose!

The heavily salted herring came from the North Sea in two hundred-pound kegs. My mother, a very strong woman, could move those kegs with ease.

Each herring had to be washed in cold water to remove the salt. They were put into a large, four-foot square ceramic pot and washed thoroughly by hand. Then they were moved to second pot and washed again, a painstaking, tedious job.

After skewering them through the eyes, they were hung outside to dry. Some of the herring were breaded and fried. These breaded herring were called bratherring. The rest of the herring were smoked.

It took a whole day to smoke one batch of fish. One person had to constantly watch the smoker because the oil that dripped from the fish into the sawdust below would sometimes catch fire.

This job was most often done by my mother and her older sister, Lucy. Nothing is better to eat than a warm herring right from the smoker—yum, yum!

*****

One day I asked my grandmother if a friend and I could ride on the back of one of the trucks for the afternoon delivery.

What harm could that do?

"Sure," my grandmother said, after some thought. "But be careful to not stand up."

As we got to the outskirts of town, we opened one of the boxes of hand cheese. They were unwrapped and approximately three inches around and one inch thick, fifty-six to a box. They were lined up in rows like soldiers.

Hand cheese is soft and falls apart easily. We began throwing them out of the back of the truck, using trees as our first targets. Then we graduated to aiming at other children.

When we got back to the factory, the driver had to account for the money he had collected versus the merchandise he had taken with him. On this particular day, he was short.

Someone came and told my grandma that they had seen some children throwing hand cheese from the back of one of her delivery trucks. She put two and two together and realized we were the culprits.

We were not allowed to ride on the trucks after that incident.

Chapter Seven
He's in the Army Now

When Germany invaded Poland, I overheard my dad tell my mother that he might get drafted and that she would have to start helping my grandmother again in the business.

Up until that point, she had been a housewife taking care of my sister and me.

When he received his papers, both my mother and my grandmother were very upset.

Several days later, my dad had a private meeting with me to explain my responsibilities for the family after he left for the army.

He was so serious that I knew instinctively my life was changing forever.

He spoke from his heart, saying, "You are going to be the head of the house now, and you will have to take on most of my responsibilities. Can you do that?"

I nodded solemnly.

"You need to take of your mother with anything that she needs. That means you will have to chop wood and make the kindling to use to build a fire in the stove so your mother can cook meals and heat the house. Also shovel snow when needed."

"What else?" I asked, trying to feel mature and responsible.

"Bring up coal from the basement when your mother needs it; potatoes and carrots, too."

"How long will you be gone?" I asked bravely.

"Very likely more than a year. You will have to watch your sister after school and help your mother make the sauerkraut in the fall."

Almost everyone made their own sauerkraut in the fall when the cabbages were harvested, chopped, and packed. The sauerkraut was so good and would last the whole winter.

We made it in a large, wooden keg. The cabbage had to be cut, salted, and put into the keg. To keep the cabbage under pressure as fermentation took place, a plate was placed on top, and a large, heavy stone was put on top of the plate to weigh it down.

After chopping the cabbages, it was stored in a large, wooden keg. The cabbage was put in layers with salt between each layer. One of us children, whose feet had been vigorously scrubbed clean, was put in the keg, usually me.

I had to walk around on top of the cabbage to compact it. This was done over and over again until the keg was close to full. Then a layer of whole apples was put on top. Sometimes more layers of apples were put between the layers of cabbage, adding to the flavor. Those apples were delicious to eat after the cabbage had fermented!

My additional chores included washing the dishes after each meal, sweeping the balcony and patio when needed, and helping my grandmother with her livestock.

Grandmother had chickens as well as geese, and I had to feed them twice a day, corn in the morning and kitchen scraps in the evening. On occasion I also had to chop off a chicken's head since all poultry was bought alive in those days.

Chapter Eight
Then Comes War

In 1941, German soldiers by the hundreds came through our city on horses pulling loaded wagons. They were going east towards Russia.

On some days we saw sixty or seventy wagons covered with canvas. No one knew what was under the canvas because most of the time they traveled by night.

During the war everything was rationed. Each person, in different quantities for adults and children, got a monthly coupon sheet. Each sheet included different coupons for sugar, butter, flour, and other, sundry goods.

My mother, for instance, might be designated a half pound of butter, and that would have to last her the whole month. Coupons could be sold to other people; the main ones that were sold were for butter, sugar, and meat.

36

The merchants had preprinted sheets of paper for each coupon. As people received their merchandise with the coupons, the merchant had to glue each coupon onto its respective sheets. In that way, each coupon was accounted for, and the merchant was able to get his next allotment of goods delivered.

Even fuel was rationed as were cigarettes and tobacco. Coupons were distributed monthly, so we had to be very careful with fuel use.

To compensate for the low supply, the Germans invented a substitute for gas. It was called "holzvergaser." Built directly on the vehicle, the platform for it sat on the bed of a truck or car directly behind the driver's side.

The holzvergaser chamber consisted of a sixteen-inch diameter and five-foot long metal pipe with a sealed bottom. It also had a lid on top that could be pressure sealed. On the side close to the bottom was a two-inch hole with a flexible gate.

We would put some paper and kindling in the top and fill it the rest of the way with wood. Then we would light the paper and kindling through the small hole.

After the wood had started to burn, we would close the lid air tight. The gas that the wood produced would run the engine. Every so often, we would have to stop to add more wood.

If we went up an incline, the vehicle would slow down because it did not have the same power as real fuel. We would have to prepare the car at least an hour before we went anywhere and carry additional wood to be able to add when necessary. A small cooker was developed for Volkswagens.

All vehicles had covers for their headlight that only had a small, horizontal slit. The purpose for this was to be less visible to airplanes. The pilots had a harder time detecting a city because all of the houses and cars were in darkness.

*****

By the time it reached us, the war had been going on for a few years. The Germans had advanced all the way to Leningrad and were close to Moscow.

Through the early, hard winter, many German soldiers died from the cold as they did not have enough warm clothing, food, or supplies.

My dad was one of the soldiers on the outskirts of Leningrad. The way that he kept alive during the cold, winter nights was to put a wet blanket over his whole body. When the blanket froze, his body warmth stayed inside. He felt that the war had been lost, so he gradually marched alone through the back of the Russian front toward Germany.

In the following weeks, we noticed more German soldiers in town. We did not know what was happening. The only radio station that we could hear aired only what they wanted us to hear. All broadcasts had been censored since the beginning of the war.

We had no idea that the Russians were already partially through Poland and were advancing toward the German border with very little resistance. We, the inhabitants of Oberschlesien, were in the strip of land between Germany and Poland, later known as "no-man's land." It belonged to Germany at this time.

Several weeks later, large trucks with heavy guns and ammunition came through town. Guns were placed on the east side of town, and trenches were dug. This was all done in preparation to protect the town.

We also saw the new German "tiger tanks" being driven from the train station, and they were hidden in the woods just outside of town.

People were beginning to wonder what was happening, and they started to stock nonperishable food in their basements.

Grandma Soppa told my mother that if anything happened we would stay with her in the basement under the factory. Cots and bedding were moved into the basement. The basement was made of steel and reinforced concrete, so we felt that we would be safe there.

We had plenty of fish and cheese stored both in the house and in the basement. We saw very few people on the streets—only people buying food and supplies to stock in their basements.

No one knew for sure, but everyone felt that the Russians were invading Germany and could not be too far away.

The husband of my mother's older sister, Tante Lucy, had been drafted a year and a half before my dad. My mother helped care for Tante Lucy's baby girl who was about nine months old.

Thomas was drafted first, Karl next, and my father in 1942.

Since Tante Lucy had her mother-in-law, Frau Zucker, to whom her three oldest were sent and a sister to care for her baby, she was also drafted to be a cook on a train that carried men to repair the railroad tracks where needed. The tracks were constantly being sabotaged so that the trains could not get supplies to the east.

And the fabric of my family continued to disintegrate, thread by savagely ripped thread.

The military took all of my grandmother's vehicles from her. They told her that they needed them to transport ammunition. She was given a paper assuring her that after the war, she would be compensated. They also took all of her inventory of fish and cheese to feed the soldiers.

Since we lived in the eastern part of town, and the defenses were being prepared toward the east, the German soldiers took over my grandmother's factory building, as well. They said that it was a very sturdy building, and they were going to use it to store their ammunition. They also put a cannon in the front yard of the factory beside the garage where the delivery trucks had parked.

We were told that we would have to leave and go to one of the neighbors, and they would have to house us. The only things that we could take with us were what we could carry—mainly food, a pillow, a blanket, and the baby carriage.

So all of the preparations that we had made in Grandma's basement were made in vain.

Mother said that we would go to the third house down. It was a newer house with double brick walls and would be a safer place to stay. On the way to the neighbor's house, we already heard gunfire in the distance.

Both my mother and my grandmother knew the people who lived in the house to which we were going. When we knocked on the door, they were surprised to see us standing there with bags of our belongings.

My mother explained to them that the soldiers had taken over my grandmother's house and factory and had told us that we would have to find another place to stay. They let us stay in a room in their basement.

We were five people—my grandmother, my mother, my aunt's baby, my sister, and me. Part of the basement where we were had a large bin filled with potatoes. My mother made a bed for the baby on top of the bin.

Some shelves along one wall had jars of preserved fruits and large pots and pans. Instead of dismantling these, the owner procured some other boards, put them on the concrete floor to protect us from its penetrating cold, and we put our blankets on top for our beds.

The family with whom we were staying also had five members: a grandfather, his granddaughter, and her three children. They made one of the basement rooms into a bedroom for themselves and another room was used as a living room. They took the mattresses off of their beds and put them on the floor. In the living room area were tables and chairs.

Since the stores were still open, Mother went to a store and bought some groceries, including milk for the baby, and brought them back to the house.

On the way back, she heard heavy cannon fire and was very frightened. She spoke with a couple of soldiers, and they told her that if she had the opportunity to leave town, to do so immediately because the German army was going to try to push the Russians back.

When she returned to the house, she relayed what the soldiers had told her. The next night, the house across the street was hit and caught fire.

We stayed for two days and three nights in that basement. The following night the house where we were staying was hit.

Chapter Nine
Evacuation

The house had gas and water lines in the basement. They were both broken; we could smell gas, and the basement floor began to accumulate water. We could not stay there any longer because we were afraid that the house might explode due to the gas leak.

We blew out the candles and prayed nothing would ignite the gas lines until we could get out. We needed to vacate the basement, but now we had ten people needing shelter.

My mother decided that she and we three children would try to get to her younger sister, Heidl, who lived about five kilometers from the city.

My grandmother could not come with us because she was not strong enough to make the trip through the snow. She wanted to stay in her own house anyway, close to her neighbors and friends.

Two feet of fresh snow had accumulated, and it was still falling. The grandfather gave us a sled to which we tied the baby carriage with some rope; inside, the baby was firmly covered and strapped.

My sister, wrapped snuggly in blankets, was tied onto the front of the sled. We tied the ends of a blanket to the sled, and I put it around my waist so I could pull the sled. My mother held onto the baby carriage handles and pushed.

When we got outside and headed out of town, we could see all of the destruction. The gun shells had been coming from a long distance. We were all by ourselves on the streets heading out of town in the opposite direction of the Russian invasion and in the direction of Tante Heidl's house.

Trudging through the snow was a very slow process. We wanted to go down the main street, but soldiers stopped us and told us not to leave—we could get killed.

My mother decided to go through the fields instead. So we went back to a point where the soldiers could not see us, and we started through the fields.

In the distance we could see a hill. My mother was very familiar with the terrain, and she told me that when we got to the top of the hill, some four or so miles, we would not have too much further to go.

I needed that encouragement because the wind was blowing so strongly that night. When the snow hit any part of my exposed face, it bit and stung.

When we got close to the top of the hill, we found German soldiers dressed in white so they would blend with the snow. They hollered at us that the enemy could see us since we had on darker clothing.

They commanded us to lie down in the snow, but my mother told me quietly to keep going. We were so exhausted from the climb and pushing and pulling the sled that our faces were red, and we were afraid we would not get to the top of the hill.

The sled kept sinking in the fresh snow, and the wheels of the baby carriage on top of the sled were covered, too. It was a very hard struggle.

My mother said that we could not stop or we would never make it up the hill.

So we kept on and on until we finally, finally made it!

At that point, I could not go any further. I lay down in the snow and was ready to quit. My mother begged me to get up, but I just couldn't. I was totally spent.

So my mother lay down beside me for a little while until we got too cold. Our clothes were soaking wet from perspiration, and the snow that had gotten into our shoes had melted.

Once more, my mother begged me to get up and move on. This time I did. Going downhill was much easier. Once we got to the bottom, the distance to Tante Heidl's house was only a short distance.

My sister had begun crying because she was cold and hungry. As we neared the one-story house, we saw a lot of trucks loaded with ammunition and soldiers all around. In the front yard was a pile of heavy gun ammunition and a large cannon.

Apparently, the soldiers were using her farm for storage, especially the two-story barn in back and the large, vacant fields around it.

When we walked through the door, my aunt could not believe her eyes.

"How in the world did you get here?"

My mother proceeded to explain that we had come through the fields and over the hill because the soldiers would not let us go down the main road.

We took off our wet clothes, and I was finally able to put on some dry clothes of my cousin, Tante Heidl's oldest boy, Frank, one of her brood of seven.

As my feet began to warm, they began to burn and tingle so badly that I began to scream.

One of the five German soldiers in the house got a bowl and filled it with snow. He put my feet in the bowl and rubbed them, one by one, over and over with the snow. When the snow melted, he went outside and filled the bowl with more snow.

He did that three times, and after the third time, the pain began to subside. When my feet were back to normal, he told me to go outside and play with the other children; who knew when we would have that opportunity again?

I think he knew that war was coming to our village, and our lives would never be the same again.

Chapter Ten
Sanity Amidst the Insanity of War

My mother developed pneumonia from her trek in the icy snowstorm. A military doctor checked her, and the soldiers began plying her with hot tea and honey and some kind of medicine. She had to stay in bed.

Meanwhile, Tante Heidl needed to get some bread baked. The baker was still baking bread for the neighbors who were still bringing him the dough.

The bread basket was a long, woven basket about thirty inches long, eight inches wide, and four inches deep. My aunt had four of these baskets, so she prepared enough dough for each basket. Then she placed the dough into the baskets for them to rise.

While we waited for the dough to rise, my aunt shooed us outside to play. We all went outside, and one of her children decided we should go into the barn and up to the second floor.

We opened the doors where the hay was lifted into the barn and stored and decided to jump out. Below the doors was a pile of straw and cow manure covered with snow.

The brave ones jumped and landed on the pile. It was fun, so we decided to do it again. Only this time, the snow wasn't as thick since we had dislodged the top layer, so our feet landed in the manure, and our shoes were full of it.

We walked through the deep snow trying to clean our shoes before we went back in the house. We got them fairly clean on the outside, but not on the inside. When we got into the house, the soldiers said that something was stinking.

When they discovered that we had manure inside our shoes, we were sent back outside to remove our shoes and socks. My aunt had a well with a hand pump, and we had to clean our shoes, thoroughly this time, and then bring them inside to dry.

By this time, the bread had risen, so we rushed to put on dry socks and shoes, and we took the bread baskets to the bakery.

The baker looked at the dough to make sure that it had risen enough. He said that it had, so he put each loaf of dough onto a flat paddle that had an eight foot handle and shoved it into the oven.

As he gave back the baskets to us, we told him that we had some more loaves of dough to bring. He told us that we had better hurry back to Aunt Heidl and get them because he was going to shut down the ovens.

We hurried back to the house, got the other loaves, and returned to the bakery. The baker told us that the bread would be ready to retrieve in about three hours.

The sourdough bread would last for several weeks, even with the soldiers staying in the house. On the way home, we put the bread baskets on our heads and tried to balance them. When we got home, some of the baskets had snow in them from falling so many times from our heads.

While we waited to return to the bakery, we watched my cousin, my aunt's youngest son, who was about three years old, playing horse in the front yard. He loved this game! He would put a rake between his legs and run with it like it was a horse.

With the piles of ammunition and the well in the front yard, he had a race course ready-made. We watched in amusement as the rake slid away from him as he rounded the corners. His nose was always running from the cold, and he would lick his upper lip clean as it ran down, again to our amusement.

Finally, my aunt told us that it was time to get the bread. So we all went back to the bakery, and the older children carried the bread home, one loaf under each arm. The bread smelled so good! Some of the loaves had split open, and the crust was crispy. We would break off a piece of the crust and eat it. It tasted so delicious—just like candy to us!

On the way back, we heard bullets flying. We told the soldiers about it when we returned, but they said that was impossible, that the front line was too far away. What they didn't know, but we discovered later, was that the Russian troops had started invading from the back of the city. All of the preparations that the

Germans had made on the east side were of no use.

My mother's fever broke, and she began to feel better. My sister and I were very happy. We had been, secretly, very worried about her.

Preparations were then made to move all the food into the basement and make some sleeping arrangements there. One room of the basement was almost completely full of potatoes—about two feet high. The sleeping arrangements for us nine children were made on the potato pile.

A large table and chairs were also taken down into another room of the basement. The soldiers helped us with these preparations, especially since my aunt's husband had finally been drafted. He was one of the last men to be drafted since he had so many children and since he owned a farm.

Once the heavier furniture needed in the basement had been moved, the soldiers decided to drive their truck toward the city to discover how close the Russians were.

They found that the Russians had broken through and were trying to encircle the city. Now the Germans had to change their entire strategy and place their cannons away from the city.

While they were gone, my aunt remembered the forgotten meat and sausages in the smoker in her back yard. She sent us children to gather it, wrap it, and hide it all under the pile of potatoes in the basement. If the soldiers found it, they would take it, keeping it for themselves.

When the soldiers returned, they began moving the heavy cannons, relocating some of the heavy guns, equipment, and ammunition from my aunt's yard. Many more soldiers arrived to help. Some of the cannons were rotated one hundred and eighty degrees away from the city toward the other direction.

We were told to get into the basement as soon as possible because the shelling could begin at anytime. We barricaded the windows in the basement by putting wood or anything we could find on the outside. We hoped this would prevent bullets from coming into the basement.

As the heavy cannon fire began to hit the city, my mother got all of us children into the basement while my aunt collected water from the well and brought it down into the basement for us.

The attack continued throughout the night and into the next day intermittently. It quieted down a little the next day. The Germans may have pushed the Russians back in that particular area, we did not know for sure, but by nightfall of the second day, it all started again.

This time, one side of the house got hit.

Chapter Eleven
Evacuation—Again!

My mother and aunt quickly left the basement and went upstairs to look around. They saw a reflection of fire through the window and thought the house was probably on fire. It was pitch black dark—the only thing that they could really see was the white snow.

The decision was made for everyone to evacuate. We would go through the pantry window which was about four feet above the floor, two feet wide and three feet tall.

Tante Heidl got a wooden box that was filled with carrots or onions and emptied it. She turned it upside down and put it in front of the window. Then she put a chair on top of the box to make it high enough to step from the chair onto the window sill. Then we had to jump about six feet down on the other side into the snow.

My aunt went through the window first. She had to locate a house where we could go because she was more familiar with the neighborhood. She had to lie down in the snow because the bullets were flying overhead, and she did not know from which direction they were coming. With the dark clothing, any movement could easily be detected against the white snow.

My mother put Tante Heidl's three-year-old through the window first, then my four-year-old sister, and then Tante Lucy's baby. We older children were able to climb out by ourselves, and Mother was the last one out of the window.

She tied the baby to her stomach with a blanket, and we crawled on all fours through the snow with Tante Heidl leading the way.

We passed one house that had a fence around it. My aunt found an opening in the fence for us to get through. That was the only way to get to the third house where she wanted to go.

That particular house had been constructed the year before and was a two-story, brick house. It was at the edge of the village and overlooked a large valley of grazing land. The valley was wide open with no trees and was at the back of the house. No trees or houses could be seen for at least a mile on each side of the valley.

My aunt knocked on the window of their basement, called the homeowner's name, and asked her to open the door. We all had been lying on our stomachs in the snow until she came to the door.

She finally opened the door when my aunt identified herself, and, one by one, we very quietly went inside and down into the basement.

When we all got into the basement, my aunt realized that her eldest son was not there. She went hysterical and wanted to go back to get him, but everyone talked her out of it.

Frank had been sleeping on the pile of potatoes under a feather comforter, and he had not heard the commotion when we left, probably since we were trying to be quiet.

When he finally awoke, he realized that everyone was gone. He searched around and found the box with the chair under the pantry window. He figured that we must have climbed out.

So he climbed out, too, and found our trail in the snow. He followed the trail through the fence hole and found us at the neighbor's house.

My aunt was very relieved and asked him how he had found us. He told her that he had not seen any footprints, but he had crawled through our pathway in snow, hoping that we were the ones who had blazed the trail.

Six people were already living in this house, a lady, her husband, three children, and a one-and-a-half-year-old baby. Then here we come with twelve more people— two adults and ten children, one a baby.

We were all spread out in two rooms in the basement, all eighteen of us: four adults, thirteen children, and two babies. The basement windows had been filled with bricks on the outside and blankets and feather comforters on the inside.

The homeowner had some sauerkraut she had made, stored in a keg. She also had a lot of potatoes. These two staples were rather standard staples for everyone.

The first few days she shared the food with us, but after that, we had to live on two potatoes and one cup of sauerkraut each per day.

We built a little fire on the floor in one of the rooms to roast the potatoes. A lot of the time, they were only half cooked, and most of the time, the adults would just wipe the potatoes and eat them raw.

The rooms in the basement were very smoky because we could not let the smoke out for fear of being found. Stored in one of the basement rooms was coal and wood which we used for heating and cooking.

At first the homeowner shared her baby food with us to feed our babies, but when that ran out, the babies were fed some mashed potatoes with butter and some water. They were fed twice a day but more often if they cried too much. They were also fed some of the vegetables and fruit that had been preserved and stored for the winter.

For the first few days, no soldiers, neither Germans nor Russians, could get to us because we were in "no-man's land.

One night, however, a grenade hit the house on one corner of the first floor.

Chapter Twelve
Death and Divine Protection

The grenade hit the house on one
corner of the first floor, exposing the
basement wall and creating a hole as the
bricks crumbled from the ceiling down. The
hole was large enough for a person to crawl
in or out.

Luckily, the hole was on the side of
the room where the coal and wood were
stored. It was the area of the house that
faced the valley, and the basement was more
exposed on this side.

Later that evening, two young
women found the opening to the basement
and hollered for someone to open the door
for them.

The old man went toward the hole.
He thought he recognized one of the two
women there, so he told them to come to the
front door, and he would let them in.

The women quickly made their way
to the basement. One woman had a child

wrapped in a big blanket and was holding it close to her chest.

She said that they had come from their house that was on fire. The rest of her family had been killed by the grenade attack—her mother, sister, and brother. The only reason that the two women had survived was because they were on the other side of the basement.

They had been running from house to house, but all of the houses had been empty, or no one would answer. The bullets had been flying around their heads, but they had kept running. And although that was not very smart because it made them more visible, they had been lucky.

They were shaking as they told their story. After they had calmed down a bit, the woman with the child began to unwrap it. Once it was unwrapped, we found that the child had been shot in the head and was dead.

The woman started screaming hysterically, tears running down her face. She began shaking the child.

All of the other women tried to calm her. They told her they would take the baby and wrap it nicely in the blanket, laying it to rest in the room with the coal and wood. They told her that it had been God's will.

She gradually calmed, but she mourned, not only for her baby, but for the rest of her family she had seen killed. The other woman was her only surviving relative.

The old man busied himself by getting some boards and whatever he could find to close the hole in the basement. The unbelievable fear we all felt was palpable.

By morning the shelling had calmed, and we were running out of butter to make the potato mash for the babies. Tante Heidl said that even if her house had been destroyed, the basement should still be relatively intact.

So at dusk that evening, Frank and I, since we were the oldest, were told by my aunt to try to get back to her house. She told us where she had hidden some additional meat and butter under the potatoes. She told us to crawl on our stomachs through the snow so that we would not be seen or shot.

When we got to her house, we saw that it had been heavily damaged. As we made an attempt to go down into the basement, we saw a lot of rubble and a burning candle in a recessed area. Beside the candle was a handgun. Someone was down there!

We went quietly into the basement. We carefully and cautiously opened the door to the first room of the basement. I had the handgun in my eight-year-old hand and was feeling quite invincible.

No one was in the room, so we moved to the door of the second room which was also closed. As we tried to open it, we simultaneously heard it squeak and saw that a candle was burning in the room.

A Russian soldier rolled out from under the feather comforters, our feather comforters that we had been sleeping under only a few days before.

The Russian soldier reached for his rifle, and I put my other hand on the handgun, pointed it, and pulled the trigger. He was down! I was shaking all over, and I could hardly move.

After the shooting, Frank and I hid because we did not know if anyone else was in the basement or close to the house. Once we were satisfied that no one else was there, we pulled the soldier off of the potatoes and began searching for the food.

My cousin started digging through the potatoes while I stood guard on the steps, looking for anyone coming, my hand poised and ready with the gun.

When my cousin found the food, we realized we did not have a container in which to put the meat and butter, so my cousin had the idea of putting them in pillowcases. The pillowcases, approximately three feet square held a lot of food, and we filled them.

Then, however, we had to figure a way to carry them while we crawled back to the house. I got the idea of tying the pillowcases to our ankles and dragging them behind us.

We had made it to where a burned out military tank was still smoking when the gunfire around us increased. We didn't know if the shots were being fired by

Russian or German soldiers since we were in a "no-man's land."

The gunfire became so intense that we crawled under the tank. It seemed like hours that the bullets continued ricocheting off of the tank above us.

Tante Heidl had crawled to the corner of the basement that was exposed, and she could see what was happening, but she was powerless to do anything other than pray that we would be alright.

We were only a short distance from the house, about three yards, but we were afraid to crawl out from under the protection of the tank.

When the shooting quieted, we finally crawled from the tank to the house. My adrenaline was so intense that I did not realize I had been shot until we were down in the safety of the basement.

I had gotten a flesh wound in my upper thigh and was bleeding. My mother cleansed my wound, bandaged it, and vowed she would not let us attempt anything like that again!

Chapter Thirteen
Stuck in No-Man's Land

Some time later we heard some Russian voices coming from outside the house. The only part of the house left was part of the chimney, part of the second floor and the four corners. The inside walls were mostly rubble.

Since the windows had been barricaded, the soldiers began trying to dislodge the bricks so they could throw hand grenades inside. We began to scream, so they stopped, and then we heard them coming toward the steps that led to the basement.

When they got through the rubble that almost completely covered the entrance and found us, the women and we children began to scream again and raise our arms in surrender because the soldiers had their machine guns pointed at us.

Only one candle lit this part of the basement, so no one could see very well. But when the soldiers opened the door, the light from the outside poured in and must have satisfied the soldiers enough so that they did not shoot.

They did, however, search through the other rooms. They saw the room where we had previously had the small fire. They told us to make a larger fire so they could warm themselves.

They had backpacks with rope for straps. One of the four wore a German soldier's jacket. They took off their backpacks and sat around the fire. Each one had a round loaf of bread and a piece of fatback which they cut up and ate. They each had a bottle of something, probably vodka, and drank it.

After they had gotten warm and had eaten, the soldier with the German jacket took off his warm hat, and her long black hair fell down. She was a woman! But she hadn't acted any differently than the other three.

One of the men went outside. When he quickly returned, they all gathered their backpacks and left. We never saw them again.

Several hours later, all hell broke loose. The German soldiers had advanced, and the Russians were forced to retreat. Unfortunately, they had not advanced enough to clear the way for us to get out of the basement safely.

The shelling lasted for about a day and a half, and by this time, we were into the second week of staying in that basement.

The Russians advanced again, and by that time, the part of the basement that we were in had been destroyed.

Again, we had some Russian soldiers come into the basement. They had to know that we were there because all of the occupants of the surrounding houses behind the front line of houses facing the Russian-occupied valley had been evacuated by the German soldiers. We were in one of the houses on the front line, stuck in "no-man's land."

Someone must have told them that only women and children and an old man were in this basement because this time, they did not bother to search any of the other rooms.

The owner's wife was a heavyset woman with a large dress, and she was sitting on top of a pile of potatoes in the corner of the room. My mother was sitting next to her, and she saw one of the soldiers take his cigarette lighter and shine it in the faces of the other young women.

Tante Heidl was in the room where the hole was in the wall. She crawled out of the hole and hid in a privy that was on its side, leaning against a pile of straw and cow manure.

My mother crawled further into the corner and under the owner's wife's dress. This saved her. The soldier looked into the faces of the young women and told them that they would have to come with him to peel potatoes to make soup.

One older Russian soldier stayed after the rest of them had gone. He spoke a little German, and he told us children that if he got some soup, he would bring some to us. Then he left, too.

The following day he returned and brought us a mess kit filled with soup. He did not come inside but handed it to us through the small hole that was left in the basement wall. Then he disappeared quickly because if he had been caught, he would have been shot for feeding the enemy.

We were very grateful, and each of us children got a spoonful of the soup until it was gone.

The next two days continued to be quiet. At the end of the second day, one of the women who had been taken to peel potatoes returned. She said that she would rather be dead than to go through what they had endured the last two days.

She said that between ten and twelve men had raped her, one after the other. The soldiers had done this to the other woman, also. She then ran out of the basement, and we never saw her again.

That same night the shelling began again.

The Russians were attacking us from the west through the large valley of grazing land. We heard machine guns being shot from the highest point left of the house in which we were staying. The Germans had a good view of the entire valley from the upper floor, and they shot anything that came through the valley.

Since the Russians could not get through the valley, they brought in tanks, and the Germans shot at the tanks with bazookas.

Later we discovered that five elite German soldiers had been keeping the Russians at bay so that the rest of the Germans could retreat with their equipment.

Three tanks that were close to the house had been destroyed. One of them was so close to the house that when it was hit, the bricks in the basement windows were blown into the inside of the room in which we were staying.

The rubber on the tank was burning and smoking, and the smoke was coming into the basement. It was so bad that we were having difficulty breathing, and we thought we were going to suffocate.

The old lady got the idea that we should take the wet diapers of the two babies and put them over our mouths and noses. The diapers were made of cotton, about three feet square.

Everyone took one corner of the soiled diapers, folded them several times to make them thicker, and breathed through them. They sure did not smell like roses, but at least we would not suffocate breathing the acrid smoke of the burning rubber!

The old man restacked the bricks into the window, and, gradually, the smoke subsided.

The five, elite, German soldiers who were in the house made their way through the rubble down into the basement. The steps were completely covered with debris. We did not know if they knew that we were there or were just trying to find a place to hide as the Russians, once again, advanced.

The first one that we saw was carrying a flashlight and was a medic. He had shrapnel wounds all over his body and was bleeding.

My mother, who was the youngest woman, wrapped him with bed sheets to try to slow down the bleeding.

The second and third soldiers had small wounds. The third soldier was supporting the fourth soldier whose leg had been blown off just below the knee. The fifth one had lost his heel on one foot and was using his machine gun as a crutch.

My mother put a tourniquet on his upper thigh. The women and older children bandaged the wounds as best they could with what they had.

The one with the missing heel must have been an officer. He told the other soldiers that they would have to remove their emblems that identified them as being members of the elite troops.

So with knives and razor blades, they removed all of the emblems that were visible on the outside of their uniforms.

He told us that their job had been to hold the Russians back in that area while the Germans retreated. Two of them had been in our house, and the rest had been in a neighboring house that overlooked the valley. That was how they had kept the Russians from advancing since they could see the whole valley.

These five German soldiers had shot out eighteen Russian tanks. After they had run out of ammunition, the Russians had been able to get close enough to throw hand grenades, and that was how they had been wounded.

One soldier said that he had one bullet left, and he had been saving that to shoot himself. We were afraid that if the Russians found the Germans in the basement with us, surely all of us would be killed.

Chapter Fourteen
The Dreaded Russians

Shortly after that, we heard the Russians trying to push the bricks and feather comforters out of the windows.

The children began to scream. Then the soldiers stopped. We don't know why they did. The only reason I can determine is that one of them had been with the ones who had come before and remembered that only women and children and one old man were left in this basement. They had no idea that now we had five German soldiers with us.

We heard the Russians coming toward the basement steps which were covered with brick and concrete rubble.

They finally got into the basement, pointing their machine guns in our faces. They began hollering on the way down, demanding to know where the German soldiers were.

The German soldiers put their arms in the air, waiting to be shot. The machine guns that the Germans had brought had been hidden.

The Russians proceeded to check the pockets and wallets of the German soldiers. Anything of value was put into the Russian's pockets, including watches and rings. The German officer could not get his wedding ring off, so the Russians cut off his finger to get it.

Next, they made the German soldiers take off all of their clothes from the waist and above. The Russians checked under the arms of the Germans for the insignia of the elite troops, which, of course, all the Germans had. This really made the Russians furious.

One of them took the shaft of his gun and hit the solder with the missing heel in the head and knocked him unconscious. Then he grabbed him by the leg, dragged him to the rubble by the steps and shot him.

The soldier who had lost his leg was very weak from the loss of blood, so he, too, was taken to the rubble and shot.

A few hours later, they took the medic and the other soldiers to be interrogated. They spent hours going through each man's wallet and their pictures. Another Russian came into the basement and said something to the others. They all left.

The following night was very quiet with not much shelling occurring. In the morning when we awoke, we were greeted by complete silence like nothing had happened.

The adults finally decided to remove a few bricks from the window and see what was happening.

My mother saw someone turning the dead soldiers' bodies over. We were not sure if he was German or Russian because some of the Russian soldiers were exchanging clothes with the Germans they killed so as not to be recognized.

The only exception between the two uniforms was that the German soldiers carried a tube on their hips that contained a gas mask. The tube was a metal cylinder approximately five inches in diameter and ten inches long.

The soldier had one of those tubes, so my mother removed a few more bricks and, in a soft voice, said "hello" in German to see if he really was a German.

He turned around toward the sound of her voice but then walked away. He either did not hear her or ignored her. When he turned over the second body, he removed the soldier's dog tags.

At that point, my mother called to him a little louder. This time, he turned around and walked toward the house.

In the meantime, my mother had removed a few more bricks. She saw that a lot of the snow had melted, and the sun was shining. A foul, sweet odor was coming into the basement.

The soldier could not believe that any people were alive.

"We have only women, children, and a very old man in the basement," my mother told him.

"You can come out," replied the soldier wearily. "We have pushed the

Russians back, but I don't know how long that will last."

So, one by one, we climbed out of the basement. We had to climb over the steps that were covered with brick rubble and past the two dead soldiers. The rubble kept sliding down as we tried to climb up.

When we finally arrived at the top, we could see that all that was left of the house was three corners and half of the chimney. We were amazed that the basement ceiling had held all of that weight and had not collapsed.

We saw all of these dead people— hundreds of them. We saw the two women who had been taken from our basement, partially clothed and dead. Women and children—all dead.

As we walked away from the valley toward the town, we could see all of the destruction, trucks, and tanks. We could see at least twenty-five destroyed tanks, two of which were German.

One German soldier had half of his head blown off with his brain hanging out. He was on his knees next to a wall. I don't know why he had not fallen over except that he must have been frozen and supported by the wall.

Shortly after, we saw more German soldiers coming toward us. They said that they would get a truck and would take us to the train station, or what was called a station, to get us out of the front line. Many others had been evacuated prior to the invasion.

They said that we must have been in a "no-man's land" caught between the German and Russian forces. We had been in that basement for over two weeks.

The old couple with us got on their knees and thanked God that all of our lives had been spared.

Finally, the truck arrived to take us to the train station. The truck had a large bed with open sides used for transporting ammunition. In fact, some of the ammunition was still on the truck.

The soldiers lifted the women and the old man onto the truck first. Then they lifted the smaller children up next. My mother then pulled the older children onto the truck. We sat on the bed, and the soldiers closed the back gate.

The soldiers had to take the shortest route which was through the fields. The way was very bumpy, and we were bouncing around like balls. We had to go over a couple of drainage ditches that were not visible to the truck driver because of the snow on the ground.

As we went through the ditches, we were thrown against each other. We did not know how far they would be able to take us. The Russians had made another attempt to advance, and heavy artillery was flying over our heads. The German front was very weak as most of the soldiers had retreated.

We got stuck in the second ditch which was larger, and we all had to get off of the truck and help push. After several tries, the driver was finally able to get the truck out of the ditch, and we all piled onto the back again.

We had to go several hundred feet parallel to the ditch to be able to find a side road to cross the ditch. We came to a forested area that had some of the treetops shot off and laying on the road. But finally, we came to a place where the tree across the road was so large we could not go over it, and the deep ditches on either side of the road prevented us from going around it.

Only one other soldier was on the truck besides the driver. A shovel and an ax were attached to the truck. One soldier got the ax and started chopping a wedge on the side of the tree closest to the ditch.

After he had almost cut it in half, they took the wench that was attached to the front of the truck and hooked it to the tree. In that way, they were able to move the tree. The driver dragged it out of the way, lowered the wench, unhooked the tree, and that gave us a small path on which to drive.

After about forty-five minutes, we came out of the forest and into a clearing. We saw several heavy German guns positioned there. The driver saw some other German soldiers and stopped to ask them for directions to where the train was.

It was not at a regular station but was stopped on the tracks, hidden by the trees of the forest from enemy eyes.

We finally got close to the area where the train was without any further incidents. Not willing to be stopped, the soldiers dropped us off at point where we could see the train in the distance. They told us to go on ahead, and we would see some soldiers who would take care of us.

We had to walk through two feet of snow, and by the time we arrived, we all had wet and cold feet.

90

Chapter Fifteen
Train Travel in War Times

Near the train, we saw a trailer, a "kitchen on wheels." The soldiers were cooking soup in a large pot that was about four feet in diameter and two to three feet deep. They were stirring the soup with a wooden paddle.

Our eyes fastened greedily on that food. Right away we were given a full bowl and a spoon. We could even come back for more as many times as we wanted!

That was the first warm food that we had eaten since the Russian invasion. They even got some milk and zwieback for the babies.

After we had enough to eat, we were told to get onto the train in any place that we could find. By this time it was late in the evening, and, to our surprise, the train was almost completely full.

No lights were on outside or inside the train. Everything was totally dark except for a small light by the soup pot.

By nightfall the temperature had dropped to about twenty degrees. The windows of the train were all frosted, and we could not see anything outside. The people were all sitting close together to keep warm. Because the train had no locomotive, it had no heat.

My mother was worried about our freezing to death, so she put us children in the luggage racks that were above the benches. She said that the higher we were, the warmer the air would be.

We did not know how long the train had been sitting there since it was so full. We were the last people to board. My mother spoke with some of the people, and they said that they had been on the train two days, waiting for a locomotive to come.

Along the other side of the train were dead bodies that had frozen to death waiting for the locomotive. The soldiers had them wrapped in white sheets, and they said they would take care of the bodies.

Finally, later that night, a locomotive came and connected itself to the cars. The locomotive's steam hose was connected to the first car. The steam then went from car to car to give some heat.

We left the area traveling very slowly. From time to time, the rails were sabotaged by removing part of the rail. The conductor had to constantly check the rails ahead of the train and be able to stop if anything was amiss.

The trains only traveled at night for fear of being seen during the day and shot at by planes. We would stop before daybreak in a wooded area and stay hidden until late the next evening.

When we stopped the next morning, we saw two train cars on the track in front of the locomotive. One was an open car, and the other was a closed car.

The closed car was closest to the locomotive and had workers in it. We did not know if they were German or Russian prisoners of war.

The open car contained replacement parts to repair the rails. These two cars were placed before the locomotive because if the rails were sabotaged, they would be affected before the locomotive.

The next evening we began traveling again. We traveled for about an hour, but then we had to stop because the rails had been sabotaged. We did not resume traveling again until about midnight when the tracks were finally repaired.

Early the next morning we arrived in Sudetengau.

Chapter Sixteen
Sudetengau and Beyond

We were all gathered into a refugee camp that was located in a school.

At this refugee camp, Tante Lucy's baby was taken away from my mother and transported to a hospital because she was sick. The authorities took all of the necessary information on the baby: mother's name, baby's date of birth, etc. My mother was told that she could contact them concerning the baby, and they would let her know when the baby was well.

At that point, we were assigned a family's house in which to stay.

The families in the area were required to take us in and give us a room that had some furniture and a stove on which to cook.

We got a room with one double bed, a table, and three chairs. They were not our property; they were only on loan to us.

We had a one-burner stove with which to heat and cook. We did not have any coal, so the stove had to be heated with wood. Fortunately, our room was near a forest, so my mother and I collected wood each day.

She carried the wood on her back, and I would drag two large limbs. My job was to chop the wood into stove-sized lengths. After several months, we had a nice-sized pile of firewood for the winter.

My mother got a temporary job in a butcher shop, but she was very homesick. We had not heard anything about my dad, and we did not know if he was dead or alive.

One day she heard that a train was going to East Germany. She packed our few belongings into a duffle bag, and we headed for the train station.

We got to the train station, boarded the train, and got as far as Deuchbrot, Czechoslovakia. The train could not go any further because of the Russian advancement.

Now we were stuck at the train station with no train leaving in any direction. My mother began to cry.

One of the conductors saw my mother crying with two small children by her side. He told her that a Red Cross train carrying wounded soldiers and officer's wives would be leaving shortly, heading west. He told her to go and ask if they could take us with them.

My mother asked an officer's wife who questioned her husband if they had enough room for a woman with two small children. He told her no.

My mother returned to us children sitting on the duffle bag and began crying again.

About thirty minutes later, the officer's wife found us and told my mother that we could get on the train, but that we would have to ride in the conductor's car which was located behind the locomotive.

Gladly my mother took the offer. The officer's wife took my mother by the hand and led us to the train. We had to cross over fifteen or twenty tracks to get to this train because it was sitting by itself.

When we got to the train, we saw that the car was meant to transport animals or cargo because is had four large windows with bars in them—no glass.

In the car were a large table, one chair, and straw in one corner. I assume the straw was there as a place for the conductor to sleep. No heat was in this car, but we were just glad to be on board.

Shortly after boarding, the train began moving. But at daybreak, the conductor abruptly slammed on the brakes. Even before the train had come to a complete stop, my mother was looking out of the window. She saw the engineer and the stoker hop out as fast as they could and run into the forest.

The conductor raced back, pushed open the sliding door, and encouraged us to jump out of the car. He then jumped out himself and rolled down the embankment.

We had no idea what was happening. The distance between the car and the ground was about four feet and was at the edge of an embankment.

My mother jumped out and went head first about twelve feet down the embankment. She climbed back up the embankment and lifted us down.

We went down the embankment and ran about seventy-five feet to a ditch. By this time we could see two "flying tiger" fighter planes that came, first on one side and then the other, shooting at the train.

Bullets flew everywhere. Some of the bullets hit the locomotive and the other cars of the train, too. After flying over three or four times, shooting at the train, the fighter planes finally left.

We remained face down in the ditch until the shooting subsided.

My mother asked the engineer, who was beside us in the ditch, how he knew that the planes were coming. He told her that the stoker, when not stoking the fire, would watch the skies with a pair of binoculars. They had been shot at numerous times before and knew what to do.

The locomotive and some of the cars had been shot very badly. Steam was coming from the locomotive in numerous places; therefore, we could go no further.

Some of the wounded soldiers had been shot, and the engineer wondered why the planes had attacked the train since each one of the cars had a large red cross on the top.

At that time, no one knew if the planes had been Russian or American, but they had been low enough to see the shark tooth faces on them.

We waited the rest of the day where we were, and by evening, a new locomotive came and hooked up to the old one. We went for a few hours and then stopped at another train station.

At that place everyone was given some hot soup. The train could not be easily seen that late at night.

We restarted our perilous journey early the next morning. Again, we were attacked by the same type of planes as in the previous raid.

Every one of the wounded soldiers who could move left the train, looking for a place to hide. They did not want to get re-wounded or killed like had happened to some of the soldiers in the first raid.

The train came to a stop on a little bridge where the door to our car was. We were unable to jump off because of a fifteen foot drop and only a six-inch space between the train and the drop off.

To give us some protection, my mother took us two children, one under each arm, got on her knees and crawled, head first, under the conductor's table. The conductor stood next to the table, holding onto it for life.

As the planes approached, they shot at the locomotive, first from one side and then from the other side. When we heard the steam coming from the new locomotive, we knew that it had been shot, too.

We saw the conductor collapse. After the planes had gone, we saw three-quarter-inch holes about eight inches apart and six inches above the table under which we had been hiding along the entire side of the car. Holes were everywhere. The car looked like Swiss cheese.

The conductor had been hit twice. The soldiers who had evacuated were reloaded, some on stretchers. We did not know if they had been re-wounded or if they were too weak.

Some soldiers came and removed the conductor's body, and we never discovered if he was alive or dead.

At midday, another locomotive came and hooked up to our train. After several hours, we arrived at a village called Bruck.

We stopped at Bruck because the American soldiers were several hundred kilometers away, and the German soldiers needed to have enough time to get the wounded off the train and into a temporary hospital.

Chapter Seventeen
The Americans Arrive

The village of Bruck had two schools that had been prepared as hospitals where all of the wounded were moved. In addition, the mayor of the village had been getting instructions from the military that he would have to provide housing for the families on the train.

We were given one room in a house where a lady lived with her eleven-year-old son. The room we were given had an iron bed for the three of us, a table, four chairs, several blankets, and a stove to heat the room.

In that house, my mother was told that she could use the kitchen instead of having to cook in our room.

That same evening, the officer's wife who had helped us get on the train knocked on the window where we were staying. She told my mother that all of the supplies were being taken off of the train, and if we could get a little wagon, she would see that we would get some of them.

So my mother and I left my sister with the homeowner, Frau Hornauer, borrowed a hand wagon from her, and went with the officer's wife to the train, which was still being unloaded.

The officer's wife told her husband that he should give us some of the supplies also. We did not know what he had put into the wagon until we arrived back at the house.

Oh my! He had given us approximately five pounds of butter, ten pounds of sugar, a one hundred pound sack of flour, a five-gallon bucket of marmalade, and a five-gallon bucket of honey.

The following day we told Frau Hornauer what we had received. We shared it all with them because, at the time, the stores had no groceries left. She had some chickens, so, in return, she gave us some of the fresh eggs when the chickens laid them.

I became good friends with Stefan, her son, who was close to my age. We played together, split firewood, and did other chores. One of our daily chores was to walk to the other end of the village to get milk.

The dairy farmer would bring milk to the stores in milk containers, and the store would sell the milk in one-liter amounts. Stefan and I would bring home one liter of milk each day.

One day on our way home with the milk, some German soldiers told us that we should hurry home because the American soldiers were on the way.

We did so, and a little later, someone ran through the streets telling everyone to put something white in his or her window, signifying surrender.

Frau Hornauer put a white pillowcase on a broomstick and put it outside one of the second story windows, but as far as we could see, no soldiers were in the streets.

The house was close to a main street, and the next morning we saw a jeep coming down the street. The jeep had a machine gun on top and three soldiers in it. They wore different uniforms, and some assumed they were Americans.

They drove through the village from one end to the other. When they saw all of the white flags, they turned around and headed back from where they had come.

Since no shooting was happening, and as nosey as we children were, Stefan and I stood in the street to watch what was happening.

On their way out of the village, one of soldiers in the jeep threw something at us. Thinking it might explode, we ran behind a wall. When it didn't explode, we retrieved it.

It was a pack of chewing gum, which, of course, we opened. It smelled so good that we removed a piece and took a little bite. It tasted sweet, so we took one piece, broke it in half, and began chewing it.

When we got home, I told my mother about the gum. She fussed at me, saying that they were enemy soldiers, and they might be trying to poison us. Stefan's mother did the same to him.

The gum was immediately taken away, and we were both made to drink a glass of milk in case it was poisoned. We were also restricted to the house as punishment.

Only a little time later, American foot soldiers came marching into the village with supply trucks following them. We did not see any heavy artillery or tanks, and no shooting of any kind occurred.

The next morning a jeep with a loud speaker on it went through the village. We were told to stay inside at all times except from two p.m. until three p.m. The stores would be open at those hours for people to buy supplies.

A week later, the time was extended until four p.m. That was the only time we could play outside.

The village was partially in a valley with rolling hills surrounding it. Two days later, we two boys decided that we would go up the hill, through some grazing land, and into the forest. This, of course, was done during our two hours of outside time.

As we were walking through the forest, we heard several gun shots. We were approximately forty minutes from the house.

When we heard the shots, we immediately hit the ground. Stefan hollered, "Ouch!" He said that his leg hurt, and it was bleeding through his pants. He took them off, and we saw that he had been shot in his thigh.

I picked him up, put his arm around my shoulder, and we tried to head for home. But his leg was bleeding badly and hurting a lot. He said that he could not walk.

I wanted to run down into the valley and get his mother, but he was scared and begged me not to go. I remembered how my mother had bandaged the soldiers in the basement and saying that if she did not cut off the blood supply, the soldiers would bleed to death.

So I took off my shirt and undershirt, and tried to tear my undershirt in half, but I did not have enough strength. I saw a mountain stone sticking out of the ground, and I began to rub the hem of my undershirt on the stone. I was able to get it started on both sides and then tear it in half.

I made something like a rope from the undershirt and tied it around his thigh, but I did not get it tight enough, and he was still bleeding badly. I redid it, but it was still not tight enough.

I told him that I would carry him down the hill, but he said that I could not carry him that far and that he didn't want to die.

Then I remembered my dad trying to glue two pieces of wood together and putting a rope loosely around them. He had tied the rope together, put a stick through the loop, and twisted the rope around the stick. That tightened the two pieces together.

So I looked for a stick that I could use to put through the loop of my undershirt. I found a limb about a foot long which I used to twist the undershirt, and the bleeding finally stopped.

I told him to hold one end of the stick tightly and not to let go because if he did, it would unwrap, and he could bleed to death. I told him that no matter how much it hurt, he was not to let go.

110

Then I ran as fast as I could down the hill, through the valley, and into the village. When I arrived home and told my mother what had happened, she told me that I would have to go and tell Stefan's mother.

When I told his mother, she started screaming and crying. She did not know how badly he was wounded and if he might die up there on the hill.

It was well past our four p.m. curfew, but I went with my mother into the street. Some soldiers were there, and we tried to explain to them what had happened, but they could not understand us.

They finally found an interpreter who understood German. He immediately took us to the American officer in charge.

With five American soldiers, one of whom was a medic, and with the interpreter and me, we left the village to find my friend. Every ten minutes or so, the soldiers had to report to headquarters because some German soldiers were purported to be in the forest.

We got to Stefan, still lying there, holding the stick. The medic told me that if I had not done what I had, my friend surely would have bled to death. He untwisted my "rig" for a short while because Stefan's leg was turning blue.

Reapplying the tourniquet and tying it to my friend's leg so he wouldn't have to hold it, we started our return through the forest and down the hill with each soldier taking turns carrying Stefan.

When we got back to his mother, the soldiers asked her where the closest German doctor was. She told them he was not too far away in a yellow building.

So two of the soldiers took turns carrying him, and with his mother and me, went to the doctor.

The doctor said that it was only a flesh wound, but he would have to clean it. The doctor took a needle, rubbed it with an iodine-saturated piece of gauze, and then dragged the needle through the wound several times. Stefan squealed like a pig because the doctor had no medication for pain.

The soldiers returned us to the house with my friend hobbling on crutches. He was told to keep his leg elevated. The second day, however, he felt much better and was walking on the crutches more easily. Stefan was a tough, young fellow.

We had to stay close to the house, but on the fourth day, he left the crutches behind and hobbled, not putting too much weight on his bad leg.

He and I went to a nearby creek that was about a foot or so deep and about fifteen feet wide with willow trees shading its banks. On one side of the creek was a nursery with green houses.

We wanted to fish, but we did not have any line or hooks. So we went back home, got some chicken wire, and made a cone out of it. We bent a willow limb around it to keep the mouth of it open and went back to the creek.

In some places, the creek was deeper on one side than the other side. One of us held the cone in the water of the deep area while the other went fifty feet up the creek with a pole to make a lot of noise to scare the fish into swimming downstream and into our trap.

When the one at the bottom of the creek would feel a bump on our makeshift dip net, he would lift it up, catching the fish.

We caught eight trout that day, and when we took them home, my mother asked us how we had caught them. We just smiled at each other and told her that was our little secret.

The following two days we had to do chores. We had to split wood by hand and bring the cut wood as well as coal from the basement into the house. But the extra chores were worth the fun we'd had catching the fish!

Chapter Eighteen
Going Home

After a few weeks, my mother heard about a palm reader nearby. She went to this person and had her palms read. My mother especially wanted to know if the palm reader knew anything about my father.

The palm reader told my mother that my dad was alive and at home, but she saw something to do with the military and that he was confined.

At that moment, my mother decided that she was going back home. The war was over by now, and the portion of Germany in which we had lived had been given to Poland.

We left Bruck with only one suitcase for the three of us. Everything else was left behind with Frau Hornauer.

We boarded a train headed for home. I don't know where Mother got the money to buy the tickets because she had not been working as no jobs were available. Perhaps she received some governmental support since my dad was in the war, and we had been displaced.

When we arrived at the train station in Katowice, my grandmother happened to be at the same train station at the same time. She had come from Rybnik to the market at Katowice to sell two live geese that she carried in her backpack.

The first thing my grandmother asked my mother was "Why have you come back?"

My mother, through tears, explained that she had been so homesick. "I did not know anyone where we were."

"We have nothing left, no house, no clothes, nothing. Everything has been taken by the Polish people," my grandmother said forcefully.

"But I was so homesick. I just wanted to come home."

At that point, my grandmother walked away and was gone.

I was shocked that she was acting that way, and my mother cried even harder.

The train from Katowice to Rybnik was so full that we could not board. A gentleman standing beside the train, however, helped my mother lift us two children, my sister first, and our one suitcase through the train window.

Neither my mother nor the gentleman who had helped her was able to board, so they both stood on the bumpers that connected the train's cars together.

When we arrived in Rybnik, we got off of the train, again through the window. Our suitcase was too heavy for my mother to carry from the train station all the way home.

So we waited on the road, hoping that someone would come who would help us, and shortly someone with a horse and buggy came down the road. He said that he was headed in that direction and would take us as far as he was going.

When we arrived at Grandma's house, we found Polish people living there. My mother asked them where her mother lived, and they told her that she had a room where the kitchen used to be. Mother saw all of Grandma's furniture, carpets, and cookware still there and being used by the Polish people.

The house had only been slightly damaged by the war and is still standing today, listed as a historic dwelling.

When Grandma returned, she was still upset with my mother that we had returned to town. Grandma told her that she was allowed to live in only one room of her own house, and to add insult to injury, she was required to pay rent.

She could hardly make a living for herself because she could not get any support or work from anywhere.

Uncle Thomas and Uncle Karl were still in the war somewhere, and they had not returned yet, so she did not know if they were dead or alive.

By the time she was finished explaining, she and my mother were both in tears again.

After staying with Grandma Soppa for several weeks, my mother had to put me into a Polish school. I don't remember if I was put into the third or fourth grade, but I did not speak or understand any Polish.

I came home the first day of school in tears because I could not understand anything that was said. My mother was frustrated and was torn about what she had done. She knew that she had to get me into school and felt that she was doing the right thing.

When I was put into the school, the teacher thought that I would know some Polish which was definitely not the case. Then they talked about putting me back into the first grade with the six-year-olds.

Grandma advised my mother to go back to West Germany. Germany had been divided into three sections. Mother had been searching for anyone going to West Germany and inquiring about what papers would be needed.

During her search, Mother saw a German lady in town who had gone to school with her and knew her by name. The lady had married a Polish man who happened to work in a military jail.

Mother told the lady that she was looking for her husband. The lady told Mother that she would get her husband to see if anyone by the name of Kuznik was in the jail. Many Germans were in the jail where her husband worked.

Mother did not hear anything from the lady for the next week. She found another classmate who had been a year ahead of my mother in school. They had a long conversation about what was happening and how things had changed for the worse.

The classmate told Mother that her house had also been taken by the Polish, and she had to rent elsewhere. The Poles who had taken over her house and furniture were even wearing her clothes, and she could do nothing about it!

She said that she wanted to leave and go to East or West Germany also, but they had so much red tape to cut through because so many others wanted to do the same thing.

A few days later Mother heard from the first classmate that my dad was in a military jail. Her husband had told my dad that my mother and his two children were safe and at home with Grandma.

My mother wrote a note to my dad asking if he could think of any way they could see each other. She gave the note to her classmate to give to her husband to give to my dad.

A few days later, my mother received a note from my dad saying that he would try to see if he could contrive something.

Because he was a trained butcher, my dad, with a military escort, would go, from time to time, to a farm to get a cow or a pig to butcher for the inmates of the jail.

He discovered that on Friday of that week, he would be going to get a cow to butcher. To get to the farm, they had to go from the city to a nearby village, and my dad did not know the location.

They procured a horse and buggy with high side walls to which they could tie the cow. They got a cow from the farmer and took it to the slaughterhouse.

After shooting the cow and hoisting it up, they began to skin and gut it. Then it was left overnight to hang so the blood would drain and it would be ready to cut up the next day.

They had to stay overnight in the village which gave my dad the opportunity to ask the two military police if he could go overnight to see his wife and children. Dad told them that he would back early the next morning.

The police discussed the matter and told my dad that they would have to have the exact address where he would be and that if he was not back early the next morning, they would arrest his wife and children and put them in jail, too.

My dad also had to give them the name of my mother's classmate who had told her of my father's place of incarceration so that my father's story could be verified.

The police discussed the plan further, and since my dad had been working with them for several months, they felt that they could trust him to do what he said he would do. They let him go, but they told him he had better return by six the next morning.

The village where my dad had slaughtered the cow was about four miles from my grandma's house. He wanted to spend as much time with us as possible, so he asked if he could borrow someone's bicycle.

Not only would that save time, but it would make Dad less conspicuous. He gave the bicycle owner about twenty slotte (Polish money) and assured him he would be back before six the next morning.

When he arrived at Grandma's house and found us all living in one room, he was very upset that the Poles had taken over and had left us with nothing.

Mother asked Dad how he had ended in jail. He said that when he had returned from the war, he had gone to the large apartment building where we had lived. Somehow that building had only been slightly damaged, and he saw all of our furniture still in the apartment.

He asked the Poles living there about his furniture, and they told him that the war was over, Germany had lost, and everything now belonged to the Polish. They said that if he did not leave, they would have him arrested.

Then he went to Grandma Soppa's factory and saw that they had changed the name to a Polish name, and he did not know anyone working there. They all spoke Polish. Although he understood some of it, he could only speak a few words.

He was looking for someplace to stay, but all of the familiar places and people were now Polish.

Someone must have seen and reported that he was a German, so the military police arrested him and put him in jail. He did not have any papers, and all people who did not have papers were immediately imprisoned and branded as "Nazis."

Dad had not seen any of us for over two years. That night no one closed their eyes because we had so much talking and catching up to do.

My parents made plans that the next time Dad was to go on a two-day butcher trip, we would run away. He told my mother to get everything ready to go at once because he did not know when the next butchering trip would be—it could be in a few days or a few weeks. However, when he did come, we would flee.

Dad left Grandma's house at five the next morning so he would have enough time to ride to the village where he should be, return the bicycle, and be back to work by six a.m.

When Dad returned the bicycle, the man told him that he could borrow it anytime that he needed it. When Dad arrived at the job, only one officer was there. The other officer had gone to spend the night with his girlfriend since Dad had been gone.

Normally, if Dad had been there, the two officers would have had to alternate watching him throughout the night. Both of them were very pleased that Dad had returned on time.

Dad got to work, cutting the cow into quarters. Then the quarters were wrapped in blankets and taken to the jail. The cook took over, cutting the meat into smaller pieces for cooking.

A few days later, we had snow, and Mother was worried that if the opportunity arose, and Dad could get away, he would have to walk through the snow and would possibly be recognized by someone who knew him.

One Saturday evening, Dad came. He told my mother that the two officers were going overnight to be with their families and that they had all agreed to meet at six a.m. Monday morning.

We left early Sunday morning. Grandma hugged us all, wished us good luck, and said that she would pray for us.

Chapter Nineteen
Escape!

We walked to the train station—
Mother and the two of us children together
on one side of the street, and my dad on the
opposite side several hundred feet behind us
so as not to raise any suspicion that we were
traveling together.

My dad wore a warm coat with the
collar turned up and a hat. The military
police were all around and were sporadically
stopping people, asking to see their
identification papers, which, of course, we
did not have.

My mother was holding both of us
children by the hands, one on each side of
her. My parents had made a plan that if
Mother saw any police who seemed to take
note, she would switch us children to the
opposite sides, and that was a sign for Dad
to keep watch. When the danger had passed,
she would switch us to the original sides.

We arrived at the train station shortly
before the train was to arrive. Mother bought

128

tickets for all four of us. We waited for the train.

Dad could not wait with us, so he went into a bathroom stall to hide, locking the door and standing on the commode so he could watch for the train. He also had to watch for the military police who were checking all the stalls for people who were hiding.

The train was delayed at least thirty minutes. Dad could not stand in the stall that long, so he came out and hid somewhere. We had no idea where, but when the train arrived, he came into the station.

We all went through the check-in area with Dad at the back. He made sure the three of us were on the train, but it was full, and he could not board, so he rode on the outside somewhere.

My parents could only afford tickets to Katowice; that's all the money they had. In Katowice, we went through several vacant, damaged houses. We were reduced to scavenging. The big search was for food.

We found some canned foods in some of the houses, and Dad found a sled.

We stayed one night in one of the damaged houses. Dad built a fire in the fireplace so we could keep warm. He got the wood for the fire by breaking up any wooden things he could find, such as tables and chairs.

The plan made by my parents was that we would load the sled with any food we found and head for the border. The roads were deserted, the fuel had been rationed, and the main mode of transportation was by train.

My sister rode on the sled, I walked beside it, and my parents pulled it. Our journey was done only at night. From time to time, we would see a vehicle coming, and we would get off of the road and hide, either behind trees or by lying in the snow.

After the vehicle had passed, we would knock off the snow from our clothes and get back on the road. After walking the whole first night, we tried to find a place to hide for the day, but we were nowhere near any houses or barns.

We were very cold and tired. My dad told my mother to try to stop the very next truck that came; maybe they would take a woman with two small children. He said that he would hide, and if a truck stopped, he would hop on the back.

A truck loaded with diesel fuel stopped, and the driver told us that he would take us, but we would have to hide between the barrels and under the canvas that was covering the barrels. My mother had to do a lot of begging, but he must have felt sorry for us—a lone woman with two, small, freezing, hungry children.

Dad was hiding behind a tree, and after the driver had covered us and jumped into the truck's cab, Dad hopped on the back of the truck, too.

Several checkpoints were on the way that stopped trucks for inspection of their cargo. We were stopped and the driver told the soldiers at the checkpoint that he was only carrying barrels of fuel. They lifted up the corners of the canvas, saw only the barrels, and let us pass.

Shortly before one town, the driver stopped and told us that we would have to get off because he could not take us into town. We got off and started walking.

We saw a little house that was under construction with a roof but no windows. It did not look like any work had been done on it for a good while.

Some straw in one room indicated that someone had been sleeping there at one time. Since we could not travel anymore in the daytime, we went to sleep on the straw, we two children in the middle and our parents on either side of us.

We went to sleep hungry because we had not had anything to eat. But we were also very tired. We slept the entire day all cuddled up together.

That evening we awoke and decided to walk several miles, searching for the next closest village. As we neared the next town, we saw some lights. As we came closer to the lights, we saw what looked like a farmhouse.

My mother was ready to give out from pulling the sled. Sometimes I was so tired that I would hop on the sled, especially when we were going downhill.

When we arrived at the farmhouse, my dad knocked on the door. Within a few minutes, an older man opened the door and asked my dad if he could help us.

Since my dad spoke some Polish, he asked the man if we could come in to get warm because we had been walking for a very long time, and we were wet, tired, and cold.

The man invited us to come in. He gave us something warm to drink and cooked some potatoes for us. He did not have much, but he shared.

He told us that he was German, but he had married a Polish woman who had died during the war.

My parents had not slept well since we had left, not even in the little house. The man told my dad that we could hide in his barn for the night so that we could get some well-deserved sleep and stay warm.

Soldiers had taken all of the man's livestock; they had left him only a few chickens. He had a son who drove a truck that transported cheap caskets to Gorlitz. The son might be able to take us that far.

The next morning his son came with a large, enclosed truck.

134

Chapter Twenty
Crossing the Polish/Russian Border

My mother begged the son to take us.

He told us that it was very dangerous because soldiers along the roads checked the trucks to see what they were carrying. He couldn't let anyone ride in the cab of the truck, but he would take the chance and let us ride in the back under the canvas behind the caskets.

As we were traveling, we hit a very deep pothole, and my mother screamed.

A young man was opening the lid of the casket and was sitting up! My mother thought that the dead were rising again!

But he was not a ghost. After he climbed out of the casket, he told us that he had stowed away in the truck when it had been parked, but he had no idea where it was going. He just wanted to get to the border. When the truck had hit the pothole, it had jolted him awake.

We arrived close to the city in the late afternoon. We had to get off of the truck quickly. The young man who had been in the casket hopped to the ground, too, and disappeared in the distance.

As we walked into the city, badly damaged by the war, our shoes and socks became wet and extremely cold from the snow.

Few people were around that part of the city, and we found a house that had been vacated due to severe damage. The top floor was totally gone, but the bottom floor was in good shape and had a fireplace. We decided to hide there.

We broke a table and some chairs for firewood so we could warm ourselves and dry our shoes and socks.

My parents began looking for blankets, comforters, pillows, or cushions—anything to create makeshift beds. They also went to some of the vacant houses nearby to scavenge for food and more blankets with which to cover ourselves.

The following day, my mother went alone to try to find some food and get information on how to get across the border away from the Polish-occupied territory and into the German territory which was now Russian-occupied.

She went to a butcher and told him her situation—that she had two small children and was trying to get across the border. She did not mention anything about my dad.

The butcher agreed to buy one of her rings. He gave her some money and a link of sausage. With some of the money she bought some milk and a round loaf of bread.

In the bakery where she bought the bread, the baker told her that he knew of a man who had a boat and was taking people across the river at night.

He drew a map for her that showed a barn next to the river where people would wait for the boater to come and transport them across the river.

Later that evening, Dad went with the map to find the barn in the daylight so he would be able to find it in the dark. It was not too far from where we were staying.

After he had checked everything and returned, he told us that we would try to make the crossing that night even though guards were patrolling both the Polish side and the Russian side.

That night we went to the barn, used to store hay. We waited and waited, but the boater did not come. Then three more people came, and we all waited longer.

The river was not too broad—only about seventy-five feet across, but it was very cold with chunks of ice floating in it.

One of the three other people, a man, said that he was going to take off his warm clothes and swim across the river. The other two agreed that this was not a bad idea. For us, that would have been impossible.

The three of them left the barn, but we stayed, hoping that the boater would come.

After another hour or so of waiting, we had not seen or heard from the other three who had left, the boater had not come, and my dad decided we had to do something.

As he cautiously opened the door of the barn, he was met by a border patrol who immediately pulled his hand gun and flashed a light in my father's face. He asked him if any other people were in the barn, and my dad told him, "No."

Because of all the footprints in the snow, the patrol knew that Dad was not telling the truth. He put the gun to my dad's back and made him walk back into the barn.

Mother almost fainted when she saw the gun at my father's back.

The patrol spoke broken German and said that the boatman had been shot the night before but had been able to get to the other side of the river. He said he would have to take us all into headquarters.

My mother begged him not to do that because she knew that they would take my dad back to jail, and who knew what would happen to us? My parents offered him all of the money they had. He took that and their watches and wedding rings, as well.

The patrolman then said he would let us go. He told us the best way to go and the places to avoid so we would miss other patrols.

Dad was not sure if he was telling us the truth or setting a trap for us. So Dad walked about a hundred feet ahead of us, stopped and listened, and then came back for us. He did that several times until we arrived at the house where we were staying.

We stayed there the rest of the night. But now my parents had no money or jewelry with which to trade or buy food.

The next day my mother went again to talk to various people to discover if anyone knew of a way to get across the border.

One lady told her that she lived close to a river that had a small, temporary, wooden bridge and was close to the border. She could see from one of the windows in her house that several times a week, patrols would stand at the bridge, checking people's papers and letting them cross the bridge, a hundred people or more each time. She was fairly certain that they would be letting people cross again the next day.

When Mother returned to the house, she told Dad what she had discovered. They decided that they would go to the bridge the next morning, and if they felt that crossing was a good possibility, we would try it.

We left at daybreak the next morning to head to the bridge which the lady had shown my mother. We found a place to hide where Dad could watch and see how the patrols managed things.

He saw that they checked the papers first and then let all of the people pass to a large gate that had a gatekeeper standing guard.

So my parents decided that the next time they opened the gate for people whose papers had been checked, Mother and we two children would walk ahead of my dad and tell the gatekeeper that my dad had the papers.

It worked! After we had passed the gatekeeper, we hurried and blended with the crowd. Then Dad ran past the gatekeeper and into the crowd to the other side.

The patrols could not shoot at my dad because of all the innocent people around him!

On the other side, we met together and quickly ran through small alleys. We came to a house that had been burned and hid in the basement until late that afternoon.

Then Dad took off his heavy coat and hat, so as not to be recognized as the man who had run through the gate, and went into the city to talk to people. He wanted to discover the distance to the Russian/American border.

When he returned, Mother went to see if she could find any aid for people who had crossed the border. She discovered that a refugee camp was close where we could get food and some money and a safe place to sleep.

When we got to the camp, we ate like pigs! We were so hungry! We also received some money and were able to sleep on some straw on the floor. The only bad thing we received there was head lice.

The next day my parents filled out forms to get new German identification papers. We stayed in that camp for three days before our new papers were ready.

By train we went to the Russian/American border. We were now in East Germany which was Russian occupied, but we wanted to go to West Germany which was American occupied.

My dad could only approximate where a town was that was closest to the American-occupied border. We traveled there by train and found a small motel that had one double bed, a table, and several chairs in the room.

Dad tried to find someone to take us across the border for a fee. The second day he spoke with someone who gave him the name of a man who had been doing that.

My dad contacted the man. He still did it, and he usually took six or eight people at a time, but the cost was two hundred marks per person, and we did not have that much money.

My dad returned and told Mother that we would have to try crossing the border by ourselves. He said he would go that evening to try to find a place where it would be safe to cross.

He was gone almost the entire night. When he returned, he said that the area where he had gone was not a good place, and he would have to scout for a place a little further. Near the place where he had been was a Russian barracks.

The second night he went again and returned at daybreak. He said he had found a place that was a good possibility. He also told Mother that not too far from the border was a broken barn with some straw where we could stay.

The following evening we heard a lot of gunfire from the direction of the border. Dad said this was the perfect time to go, so the four of us made our way toward the barn Dad had found.

After about two hours, we found the tracks that Dad had left in the snow. We followed the tracks, found the barn, and took a rest and warmed ourselves. Then it was time to keep moving.

Dad said that he would walk about a hundred feet ahead of us, and if everything was clear, he would bird whistle once. We were to follow his tracks. He did that three times, and then we arrived at a brook. We did not know how deep it was.

We would have to get across the brook without going into the water. Dad said to sit and wait for him. He would find something with which he could make a little bridge across the brook for us.

He returned with two thick boards he had torn off the barn; one was about sixteen feet long, and the other was about eight feet. We walked along the edge of the brook, trying to find the narrowest place so the longer board would span the entire width.

We found a place. Dad took the board, stood it on end, and let it drop across the brook to the other side. It made a loud noise, and we stood frozen to listen for any other noises.

After a short while, we hadn't heard anything, so Dad put the shorter board on top of the longer one. He also found a limb of a tree about six feet long and told me that I would have to cross first so that he could see how much the boards would deflect. I was to put the end of the limb into the water to use for balance.

After I crossed, he called me to come back and get my sister so she could hold onto me. I did so, and we both crossed safely.

I had to throw the limb back to the other side for my mother to use. Mother crossed alright, but when Dad came across, the boards partially went into the water. Dad was very much afraid of water because he had almost drowned as a child.

We were lucky because the half moon gave us some light. Dad finally crossed the brook, and we continued walking in the same manner with Dad walking ahead and then whistling for us when he felt it was safe to come.

At one point, we did not hear a whistle for a while. We stood very still, and all of a sudden he was there. He said we were at the border where the Russian soldiers were patrolling, right at the edge of a forest.

He said he would go ahead again and watch the soldiers. When they crossed paths and headed away from each other, he would whistle for us to come.

He left, and we waited. He finally whistled, and we went to him. Then, the four of us crossed the border together.

148

Chapter Twenty-One
A New Life in a New Place

After we had walked a short distance from the border, Dad went back, got a pine tree limb, and erased our footprints for a short distance. He didn't want them to be visible when the soldiers returned.

We continued walking as before, passing some drainage ditches. In the distance we saw a small building with a light. We thought that it must be the American border, so we walked toward the light.

When we were closer to the building, we saw that it had a large window about four feet above the ground, facing the Russian border. We stopped about a hundred feet from the building and listened for any noise.

It was a one-room building with two bunks, a table, a chair with someone in it, and another person who was putting wood in a little stove. Both of the people wore military uniforms, and we assumed them to be Americans.

Dad said that we would get close to the building, walk under the window, and pass it. We ducked under the window and kept walking. We were not seen or heard.

We came to a road that was close the building and walked into the village. Morning had just broken, and we passed a bakery. We waited until it opened at seven and bought some buns.

Mother asked if a refugee camp was nearby anywhere. We were given directions to find it, and there, we had a good night's sleep.

We were given some identification papers, tickets so we could travel by train, and orders to house us. These were given to the Mayor upon our arrival. We arrived at a village called Hattenheim, close to the Rhine River on Christmas Eve of 1945.

After reporting to the mayor, he gave us a letter to give to some homeowners so we could live in a room in their home. The mayor's wife gave us some apples, bread, and walnuts for Christmas.

A policeman escorted us to the house and spoke for us. We were given a room on the second floor of a nice villa owned by a German Russian.

The room had a forty-inch, free-standing pipe type of oven with which to heat the room. If we wanted to cook something, we had to fill it to the top with wood to have enough heat. The room had a table and three chairs but no beds, so we had to sleep on the floor.

After Christmas when the stores reopened, we were able to buy some things. We also received some items by donation.

Every day, my dad and I went into the forest to gather wood for the stove. We were close to the Rhine River, an area which has a lot of trees, so we did not have a hard time finding wood; we just had to carry it all back to the house. Most of the time, the wood was wet, making it harder to burn.

All of the vegetable fields had already been harvested except for cabbage and Brussel sprouts. At night my dad and I would go into the fields and steal some of each since we had very little money. That was our daily meal for several weeks.

Finally my dad got a job as a carpenter. The job was two villages away, and he had to walk there and back each day. He was able to bring dry wood home from the scraps that were left from his job.

One evening as he arrived home from work, he found my mother in tears and all three of us standing in front of the house. We had gone to the butcher to get some meat to cook for some soup and had been sitting in front of the house since about two p.m. It was now six p.m.

My dad began hollering for the homeowners to open the door or he would break it down. After a few minutes the lady of the house came to the door and said that she had been down in the basement and had not heard anything.

The next day my dad told his boss about the incident, and his boss told my dad that he knew how far my dad was having to walk each day to and from work—six kilometers each way. He said he would try to help us find a house closer to my dad's work.

About a week later, Dad's boss found a small house for us that was in the same village where they worked. It was in a sad state of disrepair and was close to a soccer field.

It had a kitchen, two bedrooms, a living room, and a bathroom that was entered from the outside—more like a privy.

Dad worked each day after his job to make the kitchen livable which included a stove, a sink with running water, and a door. Our table was an empty wire spool, and our chairs were empty wooden vegetable boxes.

Then Mother found a job as a maid in a butcher shop. The two incomes really helped, and the butcher would give Mother some meat and sausages each day.

Gradually, my dad and I made the rest of the house livable. My job after school was to cook supper for the family so when my parents came home from work, the food would be ready.

After school, before I started supper, I would always stop at the soccer field to play for a while. Sometimes I would start the soup and then go to play, and the soup would burn.

Mother told me that if I did not stay home and take care of my chores that she would burn my soccer shoes. On one particular day, I burned the soup again, and my soccer shoes ended in the oven!

But every chance I had, I still played even though now I had to play barefooted. I learned to kick the ball just as well barefooted as I could with shoes.

I had a very hard time in school because I had missed so many years during the war. Many times I would copy from my classmates' papers.

By the next year, however, when we went to trade school where I excelled, those same classmates were copying from my papers!

I started the apprenticeship as a staircase builder when I was fourteen years old and enjoyed it tremendously. We went one day each week to Geisenheim to a trade school where we were taught our particular trade. I was taught by one of the best staircase builders in the region.

I finished my apprenticeship and took my journeyman's exam, which I passed easily. Then I began to work on my master's. At that time in Germany, a person could open his own business if he had a master's license.

To receive the master's license, I had to work at least two years as a journeyman and pass an exam. When I was seventeen years old, I leased a piece of property very close to a railroad track, and my dad and I built a wooden building for me to use as a shop.

I built staircases for new houses, but since I did not have my master's license yet, I worked under someone else's license and had to pay him a fee. All of this was done after my regular job in the evenings and on weekends, sometimes until midnight.

Every couple of weeks, I completed and installed a staircase for a two-story house. The price I charged was between eight and nine hundred marks each. My quality of work was so much better than any of my competition that people waited to have me build their staircases.

After two years in the business, I increased the building size to store the staircases I had built as well windows, which I had also started building.

In late December of that year, I had three sets of staircases and windows for two single-family homes stored in my shop. They were to be installed after the new year.

On Christmas Eve, my shop caught fire, and the only thing I could save was my truck. I don't know how the fire started, from arson or from a spark from a passing train. No wooden structure that close to a railroad track could be insured, so I lost everything.

Not only did I lose material things, but I also lost my desire to rebuild from scratch. I was devastated.

But people encouraged me to continue and not to quit. I leased a vacant warehouse and started again. After getting a loan from the bank to buy some machinery, six weeks later I was back in operation with my master's license in hand.

Each year my business increased. I was blessed in this new area and in my endeavors. In 1955 at the age of twenty-one, I married, and we were blessed with two children.

In November of 1959 I got the notion to visit Tante Lucy in the United States. But that's another story for another day!

THE END

158

Made in the USA
Columbia, SC
11 October 2022

69239814R00091